Nibbles the Squirrel Explores Durham

**Written, Illustrated, & Photographed by
Paul Clark**

Dedicated to my family
Ann, Thomas, William, & James

Nibbles was looking for nuts in Durham today, He started at the park where kids laugh and play

Nibbles rode a bus to Corcoran Street,
The bus stopped at the Bull that was as tall as ten feet

He climbed to the top to get a good view,
"Hooray" he said "now I have two"

**Nibbles got on a train and saw a dinosaur,
There were butterflies, animals, rockets, and more**

Nibbles sniffed the air and his nose got a tickle,
He saw a big building that looked like a pickle

Nibbles looked on smoke stacks and train tracks, Then he went to Duke Gardens to look for more snacks,

The ducks at the pond pointed at a busy bee hive, "Hooray" he said "now I have five"

He looked near the water in a big pile of sticks, "Hooray" he said "now I have six"

Nibbles took a tour of the
Duke Lemur Center this week,
It is the largest in the world
and a great place to seek

At the Durham Bulls Park
the Bulls had just won,
The fireworks exploded
as bright as the sun

Nibbles saw a glimmer on top of home plate, "Hooray" he said "now I have eight"

The American Tobacco Campus lights were still on, Nibbles listened to music playing on the lawn

He danced and he looked beneath an old sign, "Hooray" he said "now I have nine"

**Nibbles thought of Durham as he curled up in bed,
He rested his eyes and his sleepy head,
He took one last look around his den,
"Hooray" he said "now I have ten"**

I hope you enjoyed the book!

Look for Nibbles in your back yard or on a walk!

Nibbles will be visiting many more cities and plans to bring new friends with him!

Draw a friend for Nibbles

Draw something for Nibbles to eat

About the Author

Paul Clark is the father of three boys under the age of 5! He recently celebrated his 10th year anniversary with his loving wife Ann. Paul and his family enjoy spending time outside and learning about the world by being an active part of it.

If you enjoyed reading about Nibbles and want to purchase more books about your local community, please contact Paul at pclark0203@gmail.com.

This book belongs to

_____

All photographs and illustrations by Paul Clark.
© 2015 Paul Clark. All rights reserved.